Table Toppers

Quilted Projects from **Fons&Porter**

Table Toppers: Quilted Projects from Fons & Porter
© 2014 Fons & Porter

FONS & PORTER STAFF
Editors-in-Chief Marianne Fons and Liz Porter

Editor Jean Nolte
Managing Editor Debra Finan
Associate Editor Diane Tomlinson
Technical Writer Kristine Peterson

Art Director Tony Jacobson
Graphic Designer Kelsey Wolfswinkel

Sewing Specialist Colleen Tauke

Contributing Photographers Craig Anderson, Kathryn Gamble, Rick Lozier, Dean Tanner
Contributing Photo Assistants Mary Mouw, DeElda Wittmack

Publisher Kristi Loeffelholz

Fons & Porter
54 Court
Winterset, IA 50273
FonsandPorter.com

Produced by:
Martingale®
19021 120th Ave. NE, Ste. 102
Bothell, WA 98011-9511 USA
ShopMartingale.com

Printed in China
19 18 17 16 15 14   8 7 6 5 4 3 2 1

**Library of Congress Cataloging-in-Publication Data
is available upon request**

ISBN: 978-1-60468-571-8

Contents

Introduction

Table toppers and table runners add color and warmth to a dining table, coffee table, or sideboard. They make lovely seasonal accents, are perfect for gifts, and offer lots of opportunities to try out new techniques and color combinations.

We're delighted to bring you this collection of some of our favorite tabletop projects. You'll find pieced designs, appliquéd designs, and some that combine techniques. There are projects easy enough for beginners, and some for more experienced quilters. Our trademarked *Sew Easy* lessons will guide you through any project-specific special techniques. All in all, we think this is a collection you're sure to love!

Happy quilting,

5

BY **Marianne Fons**

Bluebird of Happiness

Marianne chose yellow and blue for her wool table topper to match some of her favorite French dishes and linens. Make this sunny-fresh project to perk up your dining area.

Size: 22½" diameter

MATERIALS

⅝ yard yellow felted wool

16" square blue felted wool

10" square red felted wool

10" square green felted wool

⅝ yard felted wool, flannel, or cotton for backing

Perle cotton in red, green, yellow, and blue

Fons & Porter Glue Stick (optional)

NOTE: Wool fabrics in the table topper shown are by Woolylady and are 50" wide.

Cutting

Patterns for appliqué are on pages 8 and 9. See *Cutting Large Circles* on page 64 to cut the 18"-diameter circles.

From yellow, cut:

• 1 (18"-diameter) circle.

• 24 Tongues.

• 1 Circle B.

From blue, cut:

• 5 Bluebirds.

• 1 Circle A.

• 12 Circle C.

From red, cut:

• 1 Small Flower.

• 27 Circle C.

From green, cut:

• 1 Large Flower.

• 5 Leaves.

From backing fabric, cut:

• 1 (18"-diameter) felted wool circle OR 1 (18½"-diameter) flannel or cotton circle.

Assembly

1. Stitch around curved edge of each tongue using yellow perle cotton and blanket stitch (*Blanket Stitch Diagram*).

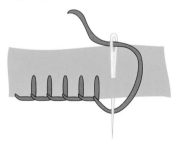

Blanket Stitch Diagram

2. Position 1 blue Circle C atop 1 yellow tongue. Hand appliqué in place using red perle cotton and blanket stitch. Make 12 blue tongues.

3. In the same manner, make 12 red tongues using red Circle C and blue perle cotton.

4. Appliqué yellow Circle B in center of red Flower, using yellow perle cotton and blanket stitch.

5. Appliqué red Flower on green Flower, using red perle cotton. If desired, trim green wool inside stitching on wrong side to reduce bulk.

6. Appliqué green Flower on blue Circle A, using yellow perle cotton. If desired, trim blue wool inside stitching on wrong side to reduce bulk.

7. Arrange appliqué pieces atop 18" yellow circle; pin pieces in place. Appliqué blue Circle and Bluebirds using yellow perle cotton, red Circles using red perle cotton, and leaves using green perle cotton.

8. Arrange tongues around yellow circle, tucking ¼" of each tongue under circle; pin in place. Blanket stitch around edge of circle, stitching through tongues.

Finishing

1. If using wool backing, pin backing circle to wrong side of table topper; slip stitch edge of circle to table topper.

2. If using flannel or cotton backing, turn ¼" seam allowance under as you slip stitch backing to table topper.

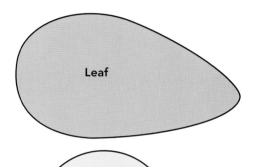

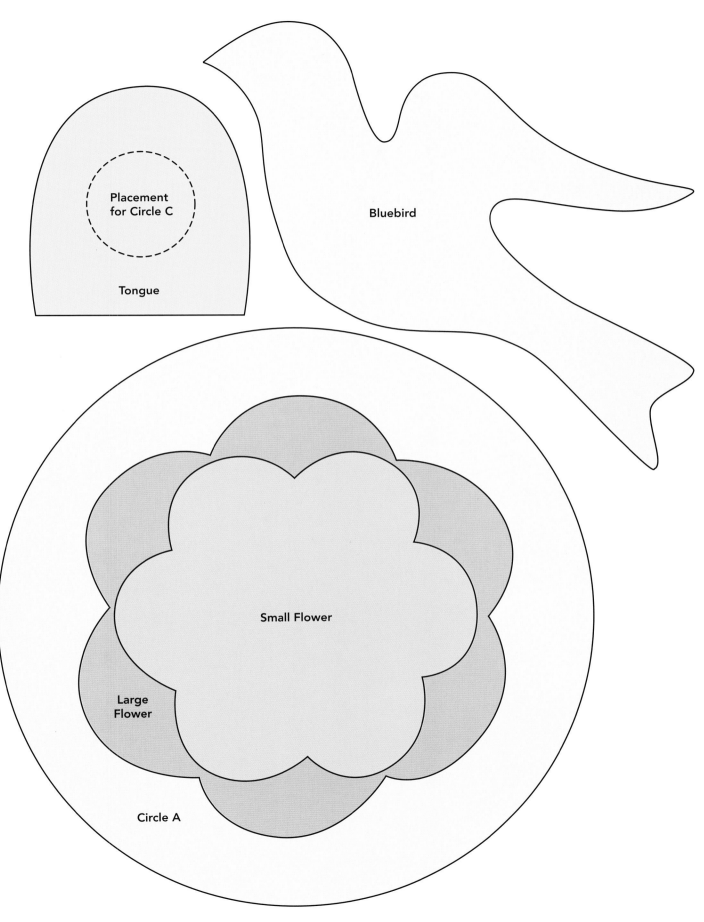

Placement for Circle C

Tongue

Bluebird

Small Flower

Large Flower

Circle A

DESIGNED BY **Jodie Davis**

MADE BY **Jayne Davis**

Candy Flowers
Table Runner

Easy fused flowers and colorful buttons adorn this cute table runner.

Size: 14½" × 38½"

MATERIALS

½ yard blue batik for background

⅜ yard light green batik for stems, leaves, and binding

1 fat eighth* medium green batik

4" × 8" rectangle each red, pink, and orange batiks

5" square turquoise batik

2½" × 5" rectangle purple batik

Paper-backed fusible web

½ yard backing fabric

2 (1⅛"-diameter) yellow buttons

2 (⅞"-diameter) mother of pearl buttons

14 (¾"-diameter) mother of pearl buttons

2 (½"-diameter) mother of pearl buttons

14 (⁷⁄₁₆"-diameter) red buttons

2 (⅝"-diameter) orange buttons

30 (¼"-diameter) orange buttons

14 (¼"-diameter) green buttons

14 (¼"-diameter) yellow buttons

2 (¼"-diameter) purple buttons

18" × 40" rectangle batting

*fat eighth = 9" × 20"

Cutting

Measurements include ¼" seam allowances. Patterns for appliqué shapes are on pages 12 and 13. Follow manufacturer's instructions for using fusible web.

From blue batik, cut:

• 1 (14½"-wide) strip. From strip, cut 1 (14½" × 38½") rectangle.

From light green batik, cut:

• 3 (2¼"-wide) strips for binding.

• 4 A.

• 2 B.

• 6 C.

• 6 D.

• 4 D reversed.

• 4 E.

From medium green batik fat eighth, cut:

• 2 each F, G, H, and I.

• 4 J.

From orange batik, cut:

• 2 K.

From pink batik, cut:

• 2 L.

From red batik, cut:

• 2 M.

From purple batik, cut:

• 2 N.

From turquoise batik, cut:

• 2 O.

Appliqué

1. Referring to table runner photo, arrange appliqué pieces atop blue background rectangle. Fuse in place.

2. Topstitch each piece ¹⁄₁₆" inside edges using matching thread.

Finishing

1. Layer backing, batting, and quilt top; baste. Quilt as desired. Table runner shown was outline quilted ⅛" around flowers and leaves and with parallel lines 1" apart in center *(Quilting Diagram)*.

2. Join 2¼"-wide light green batik strips into 1 continuous piece for straight-grain French-fold binding. Add binding to quilt.

3. Referring to photo, stitch 7 (⁷⁄₁₆") red buttons and 7 (¼") green buttons to each pink flower.

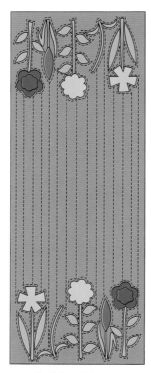

Quilting Diagram

4. Stitch 1 (1⅛") yellow button, 1 (⅝") orange button, and 1 (¼") purple button to each orange flower.

5. Stitch 15 (¼") orange buttons to each turquoise flower.

6. Stitch 1 (⅞") mother of pearl button and 1 (½") mother of pearl button to each red/purple flower.

7. Stitch 7 (¾") mother of pearl buttons and 7 (¼") yellow buttons to each stem F.

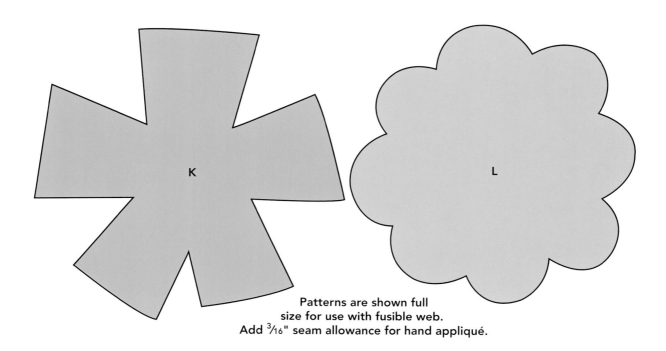

K

L

Patterns are shown full size for use with fusible web. Add ³⁄₁₆" seam allowance for hand appliqué.

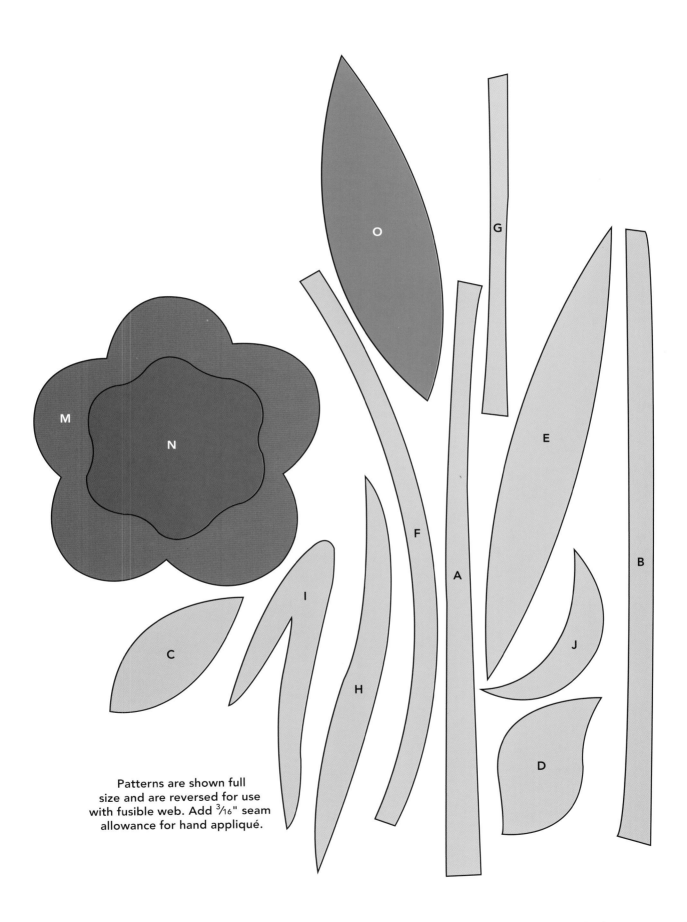

Patterns are shown full size and are reversed for use with fusible web. Add 3/16" seam allowance for hand appliqué.

BY **Betsy Smith**

Fluttering By
Table Runner

Style your summertime table with this gorgeous table runner and matching placemats designed by Betsy Smith.

Size: 19" × 55"

Blocks: 5 (9") Star blocks

MATERIALS

⅝ yard multicolor print #1 for
   outer border

1 fat quarter* multicolor print #2
   for blocks

1 fat quarter* orange print for blocks

⅜ yard orange print for blocks and
   inner border

1 fat quarter* yellow print for blocks

1 fat quarter* green print for blocks

1 fat quarter* aqua print for blocks

⅞ yard brown print for blocks and
   binding

Fons & Porter Quarter Inch Seam
   Marker (optional)

Fons & Porter Fussy Cut Templates or
   3½" square template plastic

1¼ yards backing fabric

Crib-size quilt batting

*fat quarter = 18" × 20"

Cutting

Measurements include ¼" seam allowances. Border strips are exact length needed. You may want to cut them longer to allow for piecing variations. Instructions are written for using the Fons & Porter Quarter Inch Seam Marker. If not using this tool, follow cutting NOTES.

From multicolor print #1, cut:

• 4 (4½"-wide) strips. From 1 strip, cut 2 (4½" × 11½") top and bottom outer borders. Piece remaining strips to make 2 (4½" × 47½") side outer borders.

From multicolor print #2 fat quarter, cut:

• 3 (2"-wide) strips. From strips, cut 20 (2") A squares.

From orange print fat quarter, cut:

• 5 (3½") D squares, centering design on each. If not using the Fons & Porter Fussy Cut Template, place plastic template square atop fabric; draw around template. Cut on drawn line.

From orange print, cut:

• 2 (2"-wide) strips. From strips, cut 24 (2") A squares.

• 4 (1½"-wide) strips. From 1 strip, cut 2 (1½" × 9½") top and bottom inner borders. Piece remaining strips to make 2 (1½" × 45½") side inner borders.

From yellow print fat quarter, cut:

• 3 (2⅜"-wide) strips. From strips, cut 20 (2⅜") squares.

   NOTE: If not using the Fons & Porter Quarter Inch Seam Marker, cut squares in half diagonally to make 40 half-square C triangles.

• 4 (2"-wide) strips. From strips, cut 12 (2" × 3½") B rectangles and 12 (2") A squares.

From green print fat quarter, cut:

• 1 (2⅜"-wide) strip. From strip, cut 8 (2⅜") squares.

   NOTE: If not using the Fons & Porter Quarter Inch Seam Marker, cut squares in half diagonally to make 16 half-square C triangles.

• 3 (2"-wide) strips. From strips, cut 8 (2" × 3½") B rectangles and 8 (2") A squares.

From aqua print fat quarter, cut:

- 2 (2⅜"-wide) strips. From strips, cut 12 (2⅜") squares.
  NOTE: If not using the Fons & Porter Quarter Inch Seam Marker, cut squares in half diagonally to make 24 half-square C triangles.
- 2 (2"-wide) strips. From strips, cut 16 (2") A squares.
- 4 (1½"-wide) strips. From strips, cut 16 (1½"× 2½") F rectangles and 20 (1½") E squares.

From brown print, cut:

- 1 (2½"-wide) strip. From strip, cut 4 (2½") G squares.
- 5 (2¼"-wide) strips for binding.
- 4 (2"-wide) strips. From strips, cut 20 (2" × 3½") B rectangles and 40 (2") A squares.
- 2 (1½"-wide) strips. From strips, cut 32 (1½") E squares.

Block Assembly

1. Referring to *Flying Geese Unit Diagrams*, place 1 brown print A square atop 1 yellow print B rectangle, right sides facing. Stitch diagonally from corner to corner as shown. Trim ¼" beyond stitching. Press open to reveal triangle. Repeat for opposite end of rectangle to complete 1 yellow Flying Geese Unit. Make 12 yellow Flying Geese Units.

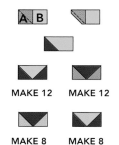

Flying Geese Unit Diagrams

2. In the same manner, make 12 brown/orange Flying Geese Units using 1 brown print B rectangle and 2 orange print A squares in each. Make 8 brown/aqua Flying Geese Units using 1 brown print B rectangle and 2 aqua print A squares in each. Make 8 green Flying Geese Units using 1 green print B rectangle and 2 brown print A squares in each.

3. Referring to *Quick Triangle-Squares* on page 60, make 24 yellow/aqua triangle-squares using aqua print and yellow print 2⅜" squares.
   NOTE: If not using the Fons & Porter Quarter Inch Seam Marker, join 1 aqua print C triangle and 1 yellow print C triangle to make a triangle-square (*Triangle-Square Diagrams*). Make 24 yellow/aqua triangle-squares.

Triangle-Square Diagrams

4. In the same manner, make 16 green/yellow triangle-squares.

5. Join 1 yellow Flying Geese Unit and 1 brown/orange Flying Geese Unit as shown in *Side Unit Diagrams*. Make 12 yellow Side Units.

Side Unit Diagrams

6. In the same manner, make 8 green Side Units using 1 green Flying Geese Unit and 1 brown/aqua Flying Geese Unit in each.

7. Lay out 1 yellow print A square, 1 multicolor print #2 A square, and 2 yellow/aqua triangle-squares as shown in *Corner Unit Diagrams*. Join into rows; join rows to complete 1 Corner Unit. Make 12 yellow Corner Units.

Corner Unit Diagrams

8. In the same manner, make 8 green Corner Units using 1 green print A square, 1 multicolor print #2 A square, and 2 green/yellow triangle-squares in each.

9. Lay out 1 orange print D square, 4 yellow Side Units, and 4 yellow Corner Units as shown in *Block Assembly Diagrams*. Join units into rows; join rows to complete 1 yellow block *(Block Diagrams)*. Make 3 yellow blocks.

Block Assembly Diagrams

MAKE 3

MAKE 2

Block Diagrams

10. In the same manner, make 2 green blocks using green Side Units and Corner Units.

Quilt Assembly

1. Join blocks as shown in *Quilt Top Assembly Diagram.*

2. Add orange print side inner borders to quilt center.

3. Add 1 aqua print E square to each end of orange print top and bottom inner borders. Add borders to quilt.

4. Referring to *Flying Geese Unit Diagrams*, place 1 brown print E square atop 1 aqua print F rectangle, right sides facing. Stitch diagonally from corner to corner as shown. Trim ¼" beyond stitching. Press open to reveal triangle. Repeat for opposite end of rectangle to complete 1 Flying Geese Unit. Make 16 Flying Geese Units.

Flying Geese Unit Diagrams

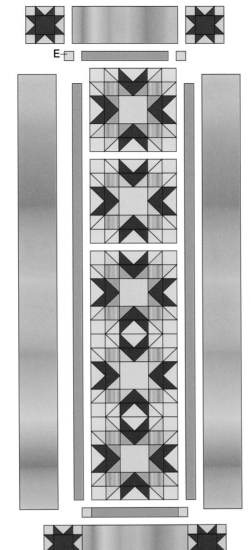

Quilt Top Assembly Diagram

5. Lay out 4 Flying Geese Units, 4 aqua print E squares, and 1 brown print G square as shown in *Star Unit Diagrams*. Join into rows; join rows to complete 1 Star Unit. Make 4 Star Units.

Star Unit Diagrams

6. Add multicolor print #1 side outer borders to quilt center.

7. Add 1 Star Unit to each end of top and bottom outer borders. Add borders to quilt.

Finishing

1. Divide backing into 2 (⅝-yard) lengths. Join panels end to end.

2. Layer backing, batting, and quilt top; baste. Quilt as desired. Quilt shown was quilted with an overall design *(Quilting Diagram).*

3. Join 2¼"-wide brown print strips into 1 continuous piece for straight-grain French-fold binding. Add binding to quilt.

Quilting Diagram

BY **Sandy Gervais**

Watermelon

Make this adorable table runner for your summer gatherings.
Who can resist the temptation of fresh watermelon?

Size: 15" × 40"

MATERIALS

1 fat quarter* cream print
1 fat eighth** green print
½ yard coral stripe
¾ yard coral print
5" square black solid
Paper-backed fusible web
⅜ yard backing fabric
12" × 32" rectangle quilt batting
*fat quarter = 18" × 20"
**fat eighth = 9" × 20"

Cutting

Measurements include ¼" seam allowances. Patterns for Watermelon and Scallop are on page 21. Follow manufacturer's instructions for using fusible web.

From cream print fat quarter, cut:
• 2 (8½" × 10½") rectangles.

From green print, cut:
• 2 Rind pieces.

From coral stripe, cut:
• 15 (1½"-wide) **lengthwise** strips, centering solid stripe in each strip. From strips, cut 150 (1½") squares.

From coral print, cut:
• 3 (5½"-wide) strips. From strips, cut 32 (5½" × 3") rectangles.
• 2 Watermelon pieces.

From black solid, cut:
• 10 Seeds.

Appliqué

1. Arrange Watermelon, Rind, and 5 Seeds atop 1 cream print rectangle as shown in *Watermelon Block Diagram*.

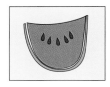

Watermelon Block Diagram

2. Fuse shapes in place. If desired, machine appliqué using matching thread. Make 2 Watermelon blocks.

Assembly

1. Join 10 stripe squares as shown in *Row Diagram*. Make 15 rows.

Row Diagram

2. Join rows as shown in *Quilt Center Assembly Diagram.*

Quilt Center Assembly Diagram

3. Add 1 Watermelon block to each end of quilt center.

Scallop Border Assembly

1. Layer 2 coral rectangles, right sides facing. Place Scallop template atop rectangles; trace around curved edge as shown in *Scallop Diagrams.*

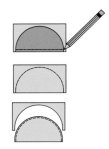

Scallop Diagrams

2. Stitch on line, backstitching at each end.

3. Trim ⅛" away from stitching as shown. Turn right side out; press. Make 16 Scallops.

Finishing

1. Position 6 Scallops atop quilt top on each long side and 2 Scallops on each end, aligning raw edges as shown in *Scallop Placement Diagram.* Baste scallops in place within ¼" seam allowance.

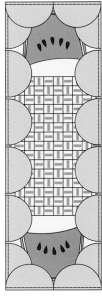

Scallop Placement Diagram

2. Layer batting, backing (right side up), and quilt top (wrong side up). Stitch through all layers, leaving a 6" opening on one side. Trim backing and batting even with edges of quilt top. Turn right side out; press.

3. Whipstitch opening closed.

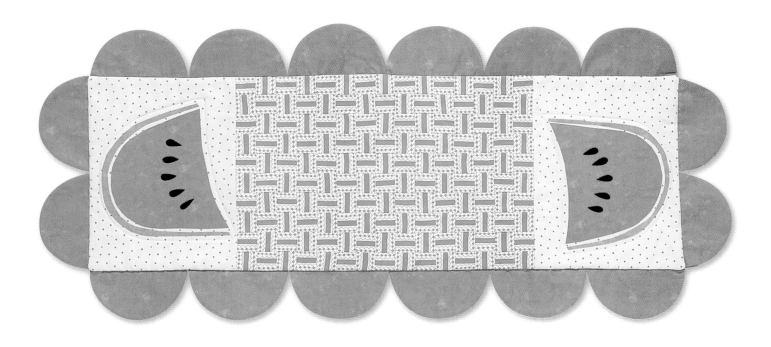

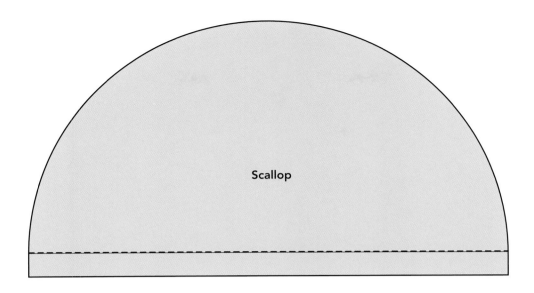

Scallop

Patterns are shown full size and are reversed for use with fusible web.
Add $\frac{3}{16}$" seam allowance for hand appliqué.

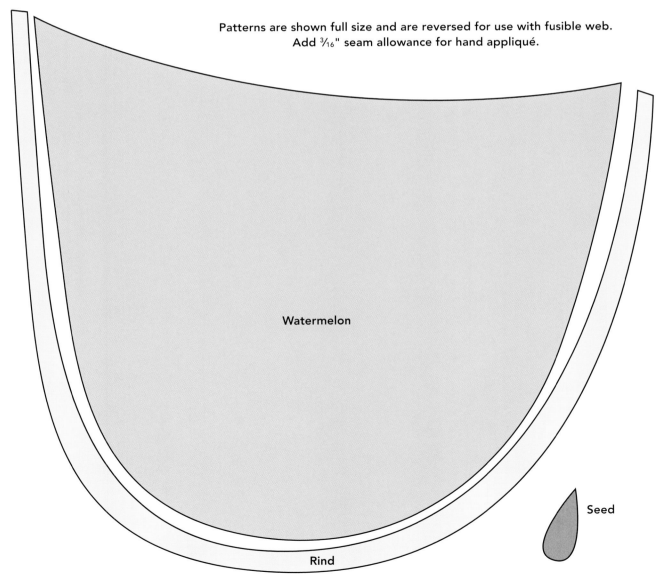

Watermelon

Rind

Seed

DESIGNED BY **Debbie Mumm**

MADE BY **Nancy Kirkland** MACHINE QUILTED BY **Anita Pederson**

Spring Daisies

Brighten your home for spring. This project goes together quickly,
so you may want to make some as gifts for family and friends.

Size: 33" × 33"

Blocks: 4 (9") blocks

MATERIALS

1 fat eighth* yellow print for blocks

⅝ yard yellow solid for borders

⅜ yard gray dot for blocks and border

⅞ yard turquoise large dot for blocks,
    border, and binding

¼ yard turquoise small dot for border

⅜ yard white solid for border and
    Daisies

Paper-backed fusible web

1⅛ yards backing fabric

Craft-size quilt batting

*fat eighth = 9" × 20"

Cutting

Measurements include ¼" seam allowances. Border strips are exact length needed. You may want to cut them longer to allow for piecing variations. Pattern for Daisy is on page 25. Follow manufacturer's instructions for using fusible web. For step-by-step photos see *Windowing Fusible Appliqué* on page 63.

From yellow print fat eighth, cut:

- 1 (3½"-wide) strip. From strip, cut 4 (3½") A squares.

From yellow solid, cut:

- 5 (2½"-wide) strips. From strips, cut 2 (2½" × 24½") top and bottom border #1, 2 (2½" × 20½") side border #1, 1 (2½" × 20½") vertical sashing strip, and 2 (2½" × 9½") horizontal sashing strips.
- 4 (1½"-wide) strips. From strips, cut 2 (1½" × 31½") top and bottom border #5 and 2 (1½" × 29½") side border #5.

From gray dot, cut:

- 2 (1½"-wide) strips. From strips, cut 8 (1½" × 5½") C rectangles and 8 (1½" × 3½") B rectangles.
- 4 (1"-wide) strips. From strips, cut 2 (1" × 25½") top and bottom border #2 and 2 (1" × 24½") side border #2.
- 4 Daisy Centers.

From turquoise large dot, cut:

- 4 (2½"-wide) strips. From strips, cut 8 (2½" × 9½") E rectangles and 8 (2½" × 5½") D rectangles.
- 4 (2¼"-wide) strips for binding.
- 4 (1½"-wide) strips. From strips, cut 2 (1½" × 33½") top and bottom border #6 and 2 (1½" × 31½") side border #6.

From turquoise small dot, cut:

- 4 (1½"-wide) strips. From strips, cut 2 (1½" × 27½") top and bottom border #3 and 2 (1½" × 25½") side border #3.

From white solid, cut:

- 4 (1½"-wide) strips. From strips, cut 2 (1½" × 29½") top and bottom border #4 and 2 (1½" × 27½") side border #4.
- 4 Daisies.

Block Assembly

1. Lay out 1 yellow print A square, 2 gray dot B rectangles, 2 gray dot C rectangles, 2 turquoise large dot D rectangles, and 2 turquoise large dot E rectangles as shown in *Block Assembly Diagrams*.

Block Assembly Diagrams

2. Join pieces in alphabetical order to complete 1 block (*Block Diagram*). Make 4 blocks.

Block Diagram

Quilt Assembly

1. Lay out blocks and sashing strips as shown in *Table Topper Assembly Diagram*. Join into rows; join rows to complete quilt center.

2. Add 1 yellow side border #1 to each side of quilt center. Add yellow top and bottom border #1 to quilt.

3. Repeat for borders #2–#6.

4. Position Daisies and Centers atop quilt top as shown in photo on page 25; fuse in place. Machine appliqué using matching thread.

Finishing

1. Layer backing, batting, and quilt top; baste. Quilt as desired. Quilt shown was quilted in the ditch and with daisy designs in the blocks (*Quilting Diagram*).

2. Join 2¼"-wide turquoise strips into 1 continuous piece for straight-grain French-fold binding. Add binding to quilt.

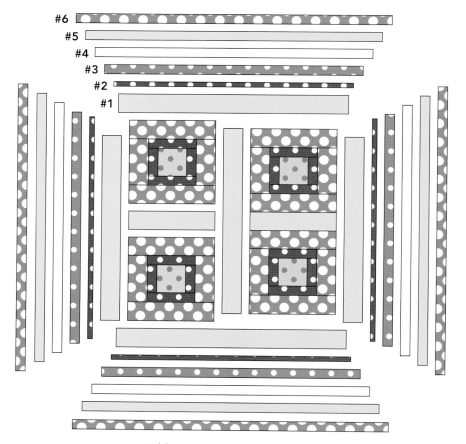

Table Topper Assembly Diagram

Quilting Diagram

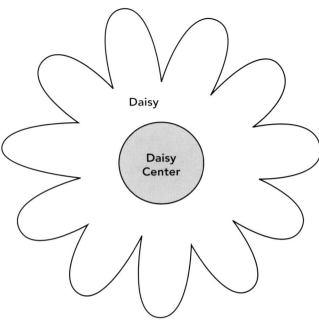

Daisy

Daisy
Center

Patterns are shown full
size for use with fusible web.
Add $\frac{3}{16}$" seam allowance for hand appliqué.

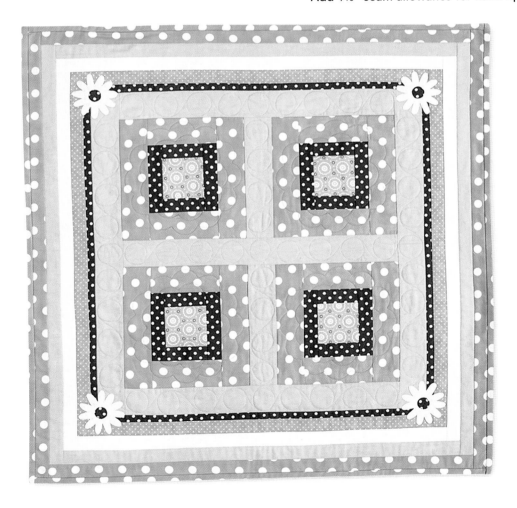

BY **Edyta Sitar**

MACHINE QUILTED BY **Julie Lillo**

Sunset Runner

This table runner, with neutral organic prints bordering a burst of color in the center, would feel at home in any style decor.

Size: 16" × 40"

MATERIALS

20 (2½"-wide) strips assorted batiks in red, purple, yellow, and orange (or 1 Jelly Roll™*)

5 (2½"-wide) strips assorted green batiks for appliqué pieces and binding

20 (5") squares of assorted beige and tan batiks (or 1 Charm Pack™**)

Paper-backed fusible web

½ yard backing fabric

Craft-size quilt batting

*Jelly Roll™ = 40 (2½" × 45") strips

**Charm Pack™ = 42 (5") squares

NOTE: Fabrics in the quilt shown are Jelly Roll™ strips and Charm Pack™ squares from the Over the Rainbow batik collection by Laundry Basket Quilts for Moda Fabrics. Precut Silhouettes for Appliqués are available from Laundry Basket Quilts.

Cutting

Measurements include ¼" seam allowances. Appliqué patterns are on pages 28 and 29.

From assorted red, purple, orange, and yellow strips, cut:

• 20 (2½" × 8½") rectangles.

From assorted green strips, cut:

• 2 Stems.

• 14 Leaves.

Sew Smart™

Purchase precut pieces to make your piecing faster.

From assorted squares, cut:

• 20 (4½") squares.

Table Runner Assembly

1. Join assorted rectangles as shown in *Center Diagram.*

Center Diagram

2. Join 10 assorted squares as shown in *Border Diagram*. Make 2 Borders.

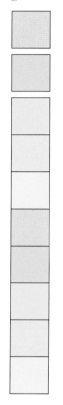

Border Diagram

3. Add Borders to Center as shown in *Table Runner Assembly Diagram*.

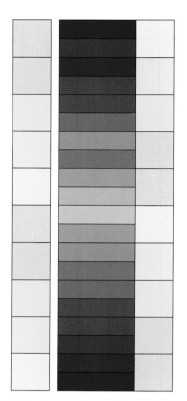

Table Runner Assembly Diagram

4. Referring to photo on page 29, arrange Stems and Leaves atop table runner; fuse in place. Machine-appliqué using green thread and blanket stitch.

Leaf

Patterns are shown full size for use with fusible web. Add $^3/_{16}$" seam allowance for hand appliqué.

Finishing

1. Layer backing, batting, and quilt top; baste. Quilt as desired. Quilt shown was outline quilted around appliqué pieces, and has an allover curvy design in center and mosaic design in border *(Quilting Diagram)*.

2. Join remainders of 2½"-wide green strips into 1 continuous piece for straight-grain French-fold binding. Add binding to quilt.

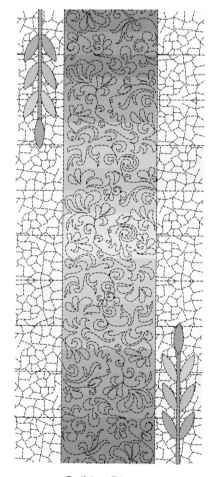

Quilting Diagram

Stem

DESIGNED BY **Wendy Sheppard**

Silver Maple

Shimmering leaves blow every which way on this appealing little accent quilt. For those new to foundation piecing this sew-and-flip technique is a fun addition to your quilting skills.

Size: 24" × 30½"
Blocks: 13 (4") blocks

MATERIALS

¾ yard blue print for blocks, outer border and binding

½ yard dark blue print for blocks and inner border

1 fat quarter* green print for setting triangles

1 fat quarter* light green print for blocks

1 fat quarter* gray print for blocks

½ yard white solid for blocks

1 fat quarter* yellow print for sashing

Paper for foundations

1 yard backing fabric

Craft-size quilt batting

*fat quarter = 18" × 20"

Cutting

Measurements include ¼" seam allowances. Border strips are exact length needed. You may want to make them longer to allow for piecing variations. Foundation pattern is on page 33. Pieces for foundation piecing are cut oversize. For instructions see *Paper Foundation Piecing* on page 62.

From blue print, cut:

- 1 (4½"-wide) strip. From strip, cut 4 (4½") A squares.
- 4 (2½"-wide) strips. From strips, cut 2 (2½" × 24⅝") top and bottom outer borders and 2 (2½" × 27") side outer borders.
- 4 (2¼"-wide) strips for binding.

From dark blue print, cut:

- 1 (3½"-wide) strip. From strip, cut 4 (3½") squares for foundation piecing (#1).
- 4 (1½"-wide) strips for foundation piecing (#8 and #10).
- 5 (1"-wide) strips. From 1 strip, cut 31 (1") C squares. From remaining strips, cut 2 (1" × 26") side inner borders and 2 (1" × 20⅝") top and bottom inner borders.

From green print, cut:

- 2 (6⅞"-wide) strips. From strips, cut 3 (6⅞") squares. Cut squares in half diagonally in both directions to make 12 side setting triangles (2 are extra).
- 1 (3¾"-wide) strip. From strip, cut 2 (3¾") squares. Cut squares in half diagonally to make 4 corner setting triangles.

From light green print, cut:

- 2 (3½"-wide) strips. From strips, cut 10 (3½") squares for foundation piecing (#1).

From gray print, cut:

- 7 (1½"-wide) strips for foundation piecing (#4 and #6).

From white solid, cut:

- 3 (2"-wide) strips. From strips, cut 28 (2" × 4") rectangles for foundation piecing (#2 and #3).
- 3 (1½"-wide) strips for foundation piecing, (#5, #7, #9, and #11).

From yellow print, cut:

- 12 (1"-wide) strips. From strips, cut 48 (1" × 4½") B rectangles.

Block Assembly

1. Trace or photocopy 14 Foundations from pattern on page 33.

2. Referring to *Block Diagrams*, foundation piece blocks in numerical order. Make 14 blocks.

MAKE 4   MAKE 10

Block Diagrams

Quilt Assembly

1. Lay out blocks, blue print A squares, yellow print B rectangles, dark blue print C squares, and green print setting triangles as shown in *Quilt Top Assembly Diagram*. Join into diagonal rows; join rows to complete quilt center.

2. Trim C squares even with edges of setting triangles.

3. Add dark blue print side inner borders to quilt center. Add top and bottom inner borders to quilt.

4. Repeat for blue print outer borders.

Finishing

1. Layer backing, batting, and quilt top; baste. Quilt as desired. Quilt shown was quilted with feather designs *(Quilting Diagram)*.

3. Join 2¼"-wide blue print strips into 1 continuous piece for straight-grain French-fold binding. Add binding to quilt.

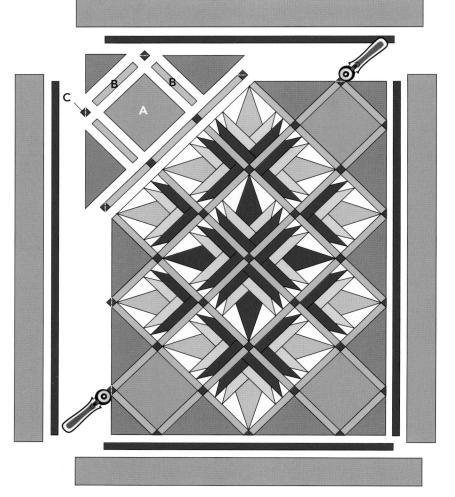

Quilt Top Assembly Diagram

Quilting Diagram

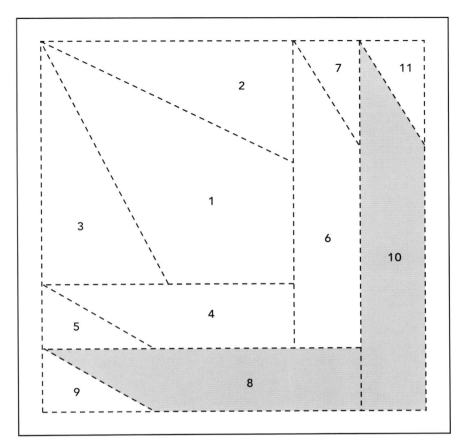

Foundation Pattern

BY **Karen Witt**

Hourglass Runner

Designer Karen Witt combined golden tans and black to make elegant hourglass blocks—only three are needed for this autumn-inspired table runner.

Size: 18" × 46½"
Blocks: 3 (10") blocks

MATERIALS

6 fat eighths** assorted black prints for blocks

2 fat quarters* assorted black prints for side borders and binding

1 fat eighth** tan print #1 for block centers

½ yard tan print #2 for setting triangles

3 fat eighths** assorted beige prints for blocks

3 fat eighths** assorted cream prints for blocks

¾ yard backing fabric

Crib-size quilt batting

*fat quarter = 18" × 20"

**fat eighth = 9" × 20"

Cutting

Measurements include ¼" seam allowances. Border strips are exact length needed. You may want to make them longer to allow for piecing variations.

From *each* of 3 black print fat eighths, cut:

- 1 (3¼"-wide) strip. From strip, cut 2 (3¼") A squares.
- 1 (2½"-wide) strip. From strip, cut 4 (2½") B squares.

From *each* of 3 black print fat eighths, cut:

- 1 (2⅞"-wide) strip. From strip, cut 2 (2⅞") squares. Cut squares in half diagonally to make 4 half-square D triangles.
- 1 (2½"-wide) strip. From strip, cut 8 (2½") B squares.

From remainders of black print fat eighths, cut a total of:

- 2 (2½"-wide) strips. From strips, cut 2 (2½" × 14⅝") top and bottom borders.
- 2 (2¼"-wide) strips for top and bottom binding.

From *each* black print fat quarter, cut:

- 3 (2½"-wide) strips. Piece strips to make 2 (2½" × 46⅞") side borders.
- 3 (2¼"-wide) strips for side binding.

From tan print #1, cut:

- 1 (2½"-wide) strip. From strip, cut 3 (2½") B squares.

From tan print #2, cut:

- 1 (15⅜"-wide) strip. From strip, cut 1 (15⅜") square and 2 (8") squares. Cut 15⅜" square in half diagonally in both directions to make 4 side setting triangles. Cut (8") squares in half diagonally to make 4 corner setting triangles.

From *each* beige print fat eighth, cut:

- 1 (3¼"-wide) strip. From strip, cut 2 (3¼") A squares.

From each cream print fat eighth, cut:

- 1 (2⅞"-wide) strip. From strip, cut 2 (2⅞") squares. Cut squares in half diagonally to make 4 half-square D triangles.
- 2 (2½"-wide) strips. From strips, cut 4 (2½" × 6½") C rectangles.

Block Assembly

1. Referring to *Quick Hourglass Units* on page 61, make 3 sets of 4 matching Hourglass Units using black print A squares and beige print A squares.

2. Choose 4 matching cream print C rectangles and 4 D triangles, and 8 matching black print B squares and 4 D triangles.

3. Referring to *Diagonal Seams Diagrams*, place 1 black print B square atop 1 cream print C rectangle, right sides facing. Stitch diagonally from corner to corner as shown. Trim ¼" beyond stitching. Press open to reveal triangle. Repeat for opposite end of rectangle to complete 1 Side Unit. Make 4 Side Units.

Diagonal Seams Diagrams

4. Join 1 cream print D triangle and 1 black print D triangle as shown in *Triangle-Square Diagrams*. Make 4 triangle-squares.

Triangle-Square Diagrams

5. Make 3 sets of 4 matching Side Units and 4 triangle-squares.

6. Lay out 1 tan print #1 B square, 1 set of 4 matching Hourglass Units, and 4 black print B squares as shown in *Block Center Diagram*. Join into rows; join rows to complete 1 Block Center.

Block Center Diagram

7. Lay out Block Center and 1 set of 4 matching Side Units and 4 triangle-squares as shown in *Block Assembly Diagram*. Join into rows; join rows to complete 1 block *(Block Diagram)*. Make 3 blocks.

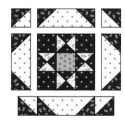

Block Assembly Diagram

Block Diagram

Quilt Assembly

1. Lay out blocks and setting triangles as shown in *Quilt Top Assembly Diagram*. Join into diagonal rows; join rows to complete quilt center.

2. Add top and bottom borders to quilt center.

3. Add side borders to quilt.

Quilt Top Assembly Diagram

Finishing

1. Divide backing in half lengthwise. Join panels end to end.

2. Layer backing, batting, and quilt top; baste. Quilt as desired. Quilt shown was quilted with a diagonal grid *(Quilting Diagram)*.

3. Bind top of table runner using 1 (2¼"-wide) black print strip. Repeat for bottom of table runner.

4. Join 3 matching 2¼"-wide black print strips to make 1 side binding strip. Make 2 side binding strips. Add binding to sides of table runner.

Quilting Diagram

BY **Debbie Beaves**

MACHINE QUILTED BY **Melissa Smith**

Dresden Daisies

Designer Debbie Beaves used her lovely daisy prints and embellished the traditional Dresden Plate block to make this special table runner. Use your favorite appliqué method—hand appliqué for a relaxing project, or machine appliqué to finish up quickly.

Size: 21½" × 48"

Blocks: 3 (8") blocks

MATERIALS

⅜ yard yellow print for block background and petal centers

¾ yard multicolor print for outer border

1 fat eighth* dark blue print for petals

½ yard medium blue print for petals and binding

1 fat quarter** light blue print for setting triangles

⅜ yard green print for scallops and inner border

1 fat eighth* orange print for daisy centers

Paper-backed fusible web

1½ yards backing fabric

Crib-size quilt batting

*fat eighth = 9" × 20"

**fat quarter = 18" × 20"

Cutting

Measurements include ¼" seam allowances. Patterns for Petal, Petal Center, Daisy Center, and Scallop Unit are on page 41. Follow manufacturer's instructions for using fusible web. For step-by-step photos see *Windowing Fusible Appliqué* on page 63.

From yellow print, cut:

• 1 (8½"-wide) strip. From strip, cut 3 (8½") squares.

• 24 Petal Centers.

From multicolor print, cut:

• 4 (4½"-wide) strips for outer border.

From dark blue print fat eighth, cut:

• 12 Petals.

From medium blue print, cut:

• 3 (2¼"-wide) strips for binding.

• 12 Petals.

From light blue print fat quarter, cut:

• 1 (12⅝") square. Cut square in half diagonally in both directions to make 4 side setting triangles.

From green print, cut:

• 4 (1½"-wide) strips for inner border.

• 6 Scallop Units.

From orange print fat eighth, cut:

• 3 Daisy Centers.

Block Assembly

1. Position 4 dark blue print Petals, 4 medium blue print Petals, 1 Daisy Center, and 8 Petal Centers atop 1 yellow print 8½" square as shown in *Block Diagram*. Fuse pieces in place.

Block Diagram

2. Machine appliqué pieces to background square using matching thread to complete 1 block. Make 3 blocks.

Table Runner Assembly

1. Position 2 Scallop Units atop 1 light blue print setting triangle as shown in *Setting Triangle Diagram*. Machine appliqué scallops to triangle to complete 1 setting triangle. Make 4 setting triangles.

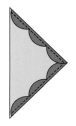

Setting Triangle Diagram

2. Lay out blocks and setting triangles as shown in *Table Runner Assembly Diagrams*. Join into diagonal rows; join rows to complete table runner center.
3. Add 1 (1½"-wide) green print inner border strip to each side of table runner center. Trim borders even with edges of quilt center.
4. In the same manner, add green print inner borders to ends of table runner, trimming ends of strips even with side borders.
5. Repeat for multicolor print outer borders.

Finishing

1. Layer backing, batting, and quilt top; baste. Quilt as desired. Quilt shown was quilted in the ditch, around appliqué pieces, and with daisy designs in setting triangles and butterfly designs in outer border *(Quilting Diagram)*.
2. Join 2¼"-wide medium blue print strips into 1 continuous piece for straight-grain French-fold binding. Add binding to quilt.

Table Runner Assembly Diagrams

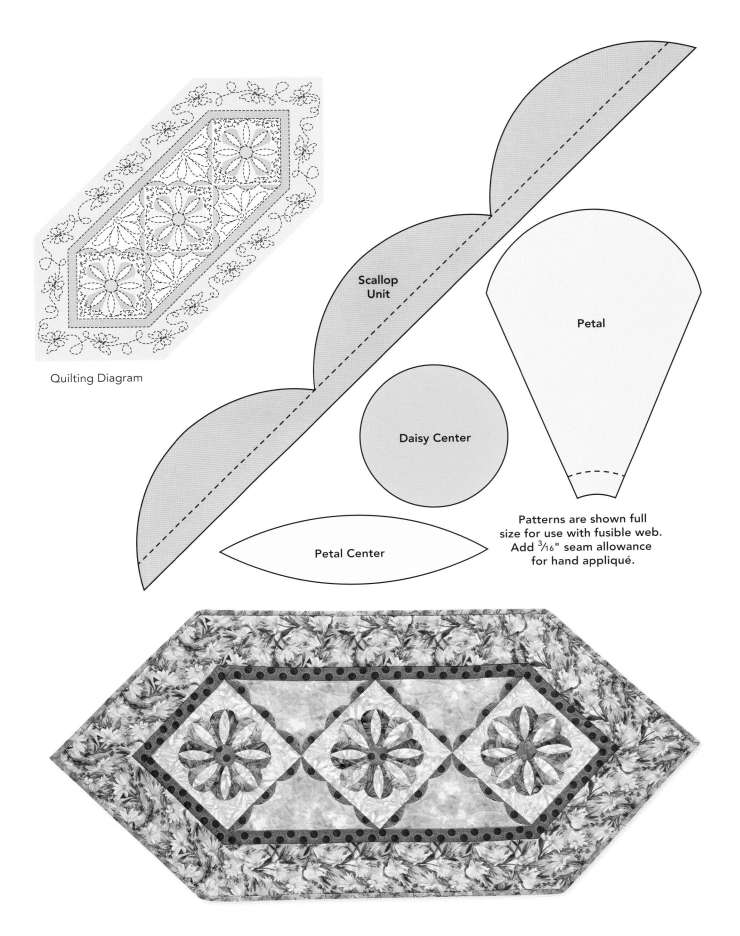

Quilting Diagram

Scallop Unit

Daisy Center

Petal

Petal Center

Patterns are shown full size for use with fusible web. Add $3/16$" seam allowance for hand appliqué.

BY **Terry Albers**

Flying South

Fans of foundation piecing—this great autumn table runner is for you!
If you're new to foundation piecing—give it a try! You'll love the results.

Size: 17" × 32"

Blocks: 4 (5") Star blocks

MATERIALS

1 fat eighth** dark teal print for
    blocks

1 yard teal print for outer border and
    back

⅝ yard green print for blocks,
    borders, and binding

1 fat quarter* orange print for blocks

1 fat eighth** black print

¾ yard gold print for background

Craft-size quilt batting

*fat quarter = 18" × 20"

**fat eighth = 9" × 20"

Cutting

Measurements include ¼" seam allowances. Border strips are exact length needed. You may want to make them longer to allow for piecing variations. Foundation patterns are on page 47. Pieces for foundation piecing are cut oversize. For instructions see *Paper Foundation Piecing* on page 62.

From dark teal print fat eighth, cut:

- 1 (3½"-wide) strip. From strip, cut 4 (3½") squares for Center Unit Section 4.

From teal print, cut:

- 3 (2½"-wide) strips. From strips, cut 2 (2½" × 28½") side outer borders and 2 (2½" × 17½") top and bottom outer borders.

From green print, cut:

- 1 (3¾"-wide) strip. From strip, cut 16 (3¾" × 1¾") rectangles for Flying Geese Unit Section 4.

- 1 (2½"-wide) strip. From strip, cut 8 (2½") squares. Cut squares in half diagonally to make 16 half-square triangles for Side Unit, Center Unit, and Point Unit Sections 2 and 3.

- 3 (2¼"-wide) strips for binding.

- 4 (1"-wide) strips. From strips, cut 2 (1" × 27½") side middle borders, 2 (1" × 20½") side inner borders, 2 (1" × 13½") top and bottom middle borders, and 2 (1" × 6½") top and bottom inner borders.

From orange print fat quarter, cut:

- 2 (3¾"-wide) strips. From strips, cut 16 (3¾" × 1¾") rectangles for Flying Geese Unit Section 7.

- 2 (2½"-wide) strips. From strips, cut 8 (2½") squares. Cut squares in half diagonally to make 16 half-square triangles for Side Unit, Center Unit, and Point Unit Sections 2 and 3.

From black print fat eighth, cut:

- 2 (3¾"-wide) strips. From strips, cut 16 (3¾" × 1¾") rectangles for Flying Geese Unit Section 1.

From gold print, cut:
- 1 (3½"-wide) strip. From strip, cut 2 (3½" × 9½") A rectangles.
- 1 (3¼"-wide) strip. From strip, cut 16 (3¼" × 2") rectangles for Side Unit, Center Unit, and Point Unit Section 1.
- 5 (2½"-wide) strips. From strips, cut 96 (2½" × 1¾") rectangles for Flying Geese Unit Sections 2, 3, 5, 6, 8, and 9.
- 1 (2"-wide) strip. From strip, cut 16 (2") squares for Side Unit Sections 4 and 5.

Star Block Assembly

1. Trace or photocopy 8 Side Unit Foundations, 4 Center Unit Foundations, and 4 Point Unit Foundations from patterns on page 47.

2. Referring to *Star Unit Diagrams,* foundation piece units in numerical order. Make 4 Side Units, 2 Center Units, and 2 Point Units with green print in sections 2 and 3. Make 4 Side Units, 2 Center Units, and 2 Point Units with orange print in sections 2 and 3.

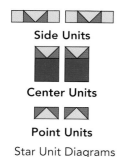

Side Units

Center Units

Point Units

Star Unit Diagrams

3. Lay out 2 matching Side Units, 1 Center Unit, and 1 Point Unit as shown in *Block Assembly Diagram.* Join into rows; join rows to complete 1 Star block *(Block Diagram).* Make 4 blocks.

Block Assembly Diagram

Block Diagram

Center Assembly

1. Join blocks as shown in *Center Diagram.*

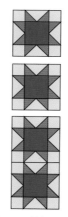

Center Diagram

2. Referring to *Quilt Top Assembly Diagram,* add green print side inner borders to quilt center. Add green print top and bottom inner borders to complete quilt center.

Pieced Border Assembly

1. Trace or photocopy 16 Flying Geese Unit Foundations from pattern on page 47.

2. Referring to *Flying Geese Unit Diagram,* foundation piece units in numerical order. Make 16 Flying Geese Units with black print in section 1, green print in section 4, and orange print in section 7.

Flying Geese Unit Diagram

3. Join 6 Flying Geese Units and 1 gold print A rectangle to make 1 pieced side border as shown in *Pieced Border Diagrams.* Make 2 pieced side borders.

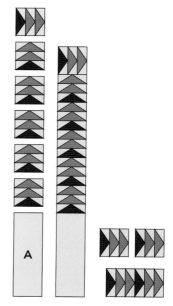

Side Borders   **Top & Bottom Borders**

Pieced Border Diagrams

4. Join 2 Flying Geese Units to make pieced top border. Repeat for pieced bottom border.

Quilt Assembly

1. Referring to *Quilt Top Assembly Diagram,* add pieced top and bottom borders to quilt center. Add pieced side borders to quilt.

2. Add green print side middle borders to quilt center. Add green print top and bottom middle borders to quilt.

3. Repeat for dark teal print outer borders.

Finishing

1. Layer backing, batting, and quilt top; baste. Quilt as desired. Quilt shown was quilted in the ditch, with straight lines in pieced border, and with a vine-and-leaf design in outer border *(Quilting Diagram)*.

3. Join 2¼"-wide green print strips into 1 continuous piece for straight-grain French-fold binding. Add binding to quilt.

Quilt Top Assembly Diagram

Quilting Diagram

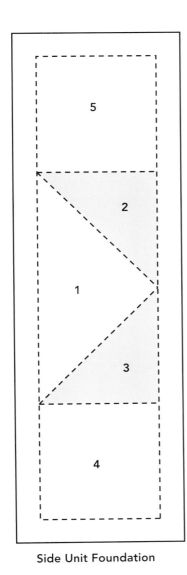

Side Unit Foundation

Center Unit Foundation

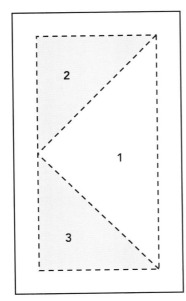

Point Unit Foundation

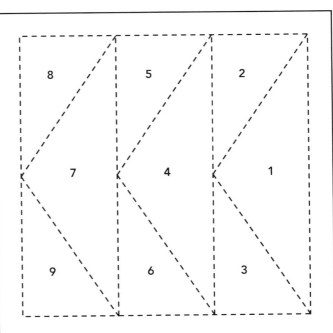

Flying Geese Unit Foundation

BY **Kelly Mueller**

Pumpkin Patch
Table Runner and Hot Pad

Make this matching set for your autumn table. Machine appliqué using fusible web and blanket stitch, and get it done in no time!

Table Runner Size: 33½" × 16½"
Hot Pad Size: 8½" × 8½"

MATERIALS

NOTE: Materials listed are enough to make table runner and hot pad.

3 fat quarters** assorted beige and cream prints

¼ yard dark green print for leaves, inner border, and vines

⅜ yard light rust print for outer border

4 fat eighths* assorted dark rust prints for pumpkins and hot pad inner border

⅜ yard medium green print for scrappy border and table runner binding

6" square dark brown print for stems

5" × 10" rectangle light brown print for corn husks

8" square light tan print for corn cob

8" square tan print for pieced borders

½ yard backing fabric for table runner

10" square backing fabric for hot pad

18" × 35" rectangle quilt batting for table runner

10" square insulated batting for hot pad

Paper-backed fusible web

*fat eighth = 9" × 20"
**fat quarter = 18" × 20"

Cutting

Measurements include ¼" seam allowances. Border strips are exact length needed. You may want to make them longer to allow for piecing variations. Patterns for appliqué are on pages 52–53. Follow manufacturer's instructions for using fusible web. For step-by-step photos see *Windowing Fusible Appliqué* on page 63.

NOTE: Cutting instructions are for both table runner and hot pad.

From each beige and cream print fat quarter, cut:

- 3 (3"-wide) strips. From strips, cut 15 (3") squares.

From dark green print, cut:

- 1 (2¼"-wide) strip for hot pad binding.
- 2 (1½"-wide) strips. From strips, cut 2 (1½" × 25½") top and bottom inner borders and 2 (1½" × 12½") side inner borders.
- 9 Leaves.
- 2 Vines.

From light rust print, cut:
- 3 (2½"-wide) strips. From strips, cut 2 (2½" × 29½") top and bottom outer borders and 2 (2½" × 16½") side outer borders.
- 3 E.
- 3 F.

From dark rust print #1 fat eighth, cut:
- 2 A.

From dark rust print #2 fat eighth, cut:
- 2 B.
- 2 C.

From dark rust print #3 fat eighth, cut:
- 3 D.

From dark rust print #4 fat eighth, cut:
- 2 (1"-wide) strips. From strips, cut 2 (1" × 6½") top and bottom inner borders and 2 (1" × 5½") side inner borders.

From medium green print, cut:
- 3 (2¼"-wide) strips for table runner binding.

From light brown print, cut:
- 2 Corn Husk A.
- 2 Corn Husk B.

From dark brown print, cut:
- 2 Large Stems.
- 3 Small Stems.

From light tan print, cut:
- 2 Corn Cobs.

From tan print, cut:
- 17 (1½") squares.

From remainders of brown, rust, and medium green prints, cut:
- 35 (1½") squares.
- 16 (⅜") squares for corn kernels.

  NOTE: Apply fusible web before cutting corn kernels.

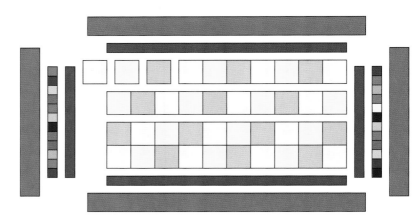

Table Runner Assembly Diagram

Table Runner Assembly

1. Lay out 40 beige and cream print 3" squares as shown in *Table Runner Assembly Diagram*. Join into rows; join rows to complete table runner center.

2. Add dark green print top and bottom inner borders to center. Add side inner borders to center.

3. Join 12 assorted 1½" squares to make 1 middle border. Make 2 middle borders. Add to sides of table runner.

4. Add light rust print top and bottom outer borders to table runner. Add side outer borders.

Hot Pad Assembly

1. Join 4 beige and cream print 3" squares as shown in *Hot Pad Assembly Diagram*. Join into rows; join rows to complete hot pad center.

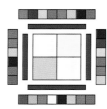

Hot Pad Assembly Diagram

2. Add dark rust print #4 side inner borders to hot pad center. Add dark rust print #4 top and bottom inner borders.

3. Join 6 assorted 1½" squares to make 1 side border. Make 2 side borders. Add to sides of hot pad.

4. Join 8 assorted 1½" squares to make top border. Repeat for bottom border. Add borders to hot pad.

Appliqué

1. Arrange appliqué pieces atop table runner and hot pad as shown in photo on page 51. Fuse in place.

2. Machine appliqué using matching thread.

Finishing

1. Layer backing rectangle, batting rectangle, and table runner top; baste. Quilt as desired. Table runner shown was quilted in the ditch around borders and with meandering in center and outer border *(Table Runner Quilting Diagram).*

Table Runner Quilting Diagram

2. Layer backing square, batting square, and hot pad top; baste. Quilt as desired. Hot pad shown was quilted in the ditch around borders and with meandering in center background *(Hot Pad Quilting Diagram).*

Hot Pad Quilting Diagram

3. Join 2¼"-wide medium green print strips into 1 continuous piece for straight-grain French-fold binding. Add binding to table runner.

4. Add 2¼"-wide dark green print binding strip to hot pad.

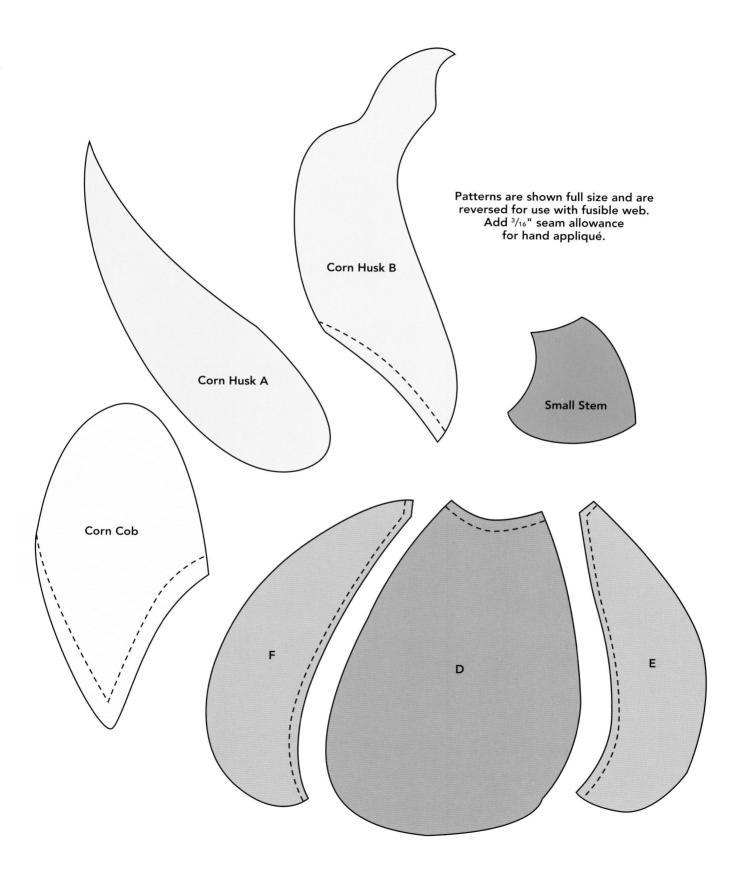

Corn Husk A

Corn Husk B

Patterns are shown full size and are
reversed for use with fusible web.
Add $^3/_{16}$" seam allowance
for hand appliqué.

Small Stem

Corn Cob

F

D

E

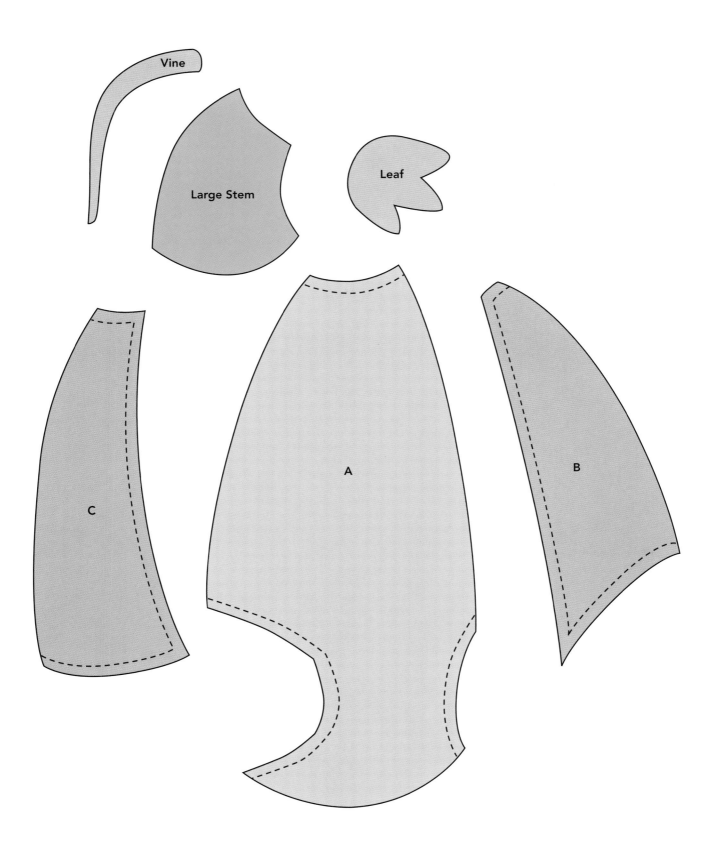

Vine

Large Stem

Leaf

C

A

B

BY **Sue Marsh**

O Christmas Tree

This fun and festive table topper, made in non-traditional Christmas colors, will add sparkle to your holiday decorating.

Size: 16½" Diameter

MATERIALS

1 fat quarter* blue print for background

⅜ yard green stripe for 1 tree and binding

3 (6") squares assorted pink prints for trees

2 (6") squares assorted purple prints for trees

2 (6") squares assorted green prints for trees

1 (6") square yellow solid for stars

1 (4") square brown solid for tree trunks

Paper-backed fusible web

1 fat quarter* backing fabric

18" square quilt batting

*fat quarter = 18" × 20"

Cutting

Measurements include ¼" seam allowances. Patterns for appliqué are on page 56. Follow manufacturer's instructions for using fusible web. For step-by-step photos see *Windowing Fusible Appliqué* on page 63.

From blue print, cut:

• 1 (16½"-diameter) circle.

  NOTE: See *Cutting Large Circles* on page 64.

From green stripe, cut:

• 64" of 2¼"-wide bias strips. Join strips to make bias binding.

• 1 Tree.

From pink, purple, and green squares, cut a total of:

• 7 Trees.

From yellow solid, cut:

• 8 Stars.

From brown solid, cut:

• 8 Trunks.

Quilt Assembly

1. Fold blue print background circle in half, then in half again. Lightly press folds to make placement lines for appliqué.

2. Referring to photo on page 57 and *Table Topper Diagram*, use creases as guides to arrange Trees, Trunks, and Stars atop circle. Fuse in place.

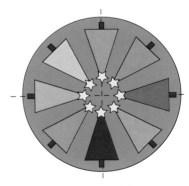

Table Topper Diagram

3. Machine appliqué using matching thread.

Finishing

1. Layer backing, batting, and table topper top; baste. Quilt as desired. Quilt shown was quilted with meandering in background *(Quilting Diagram)*.

2. Add binding to table topper.

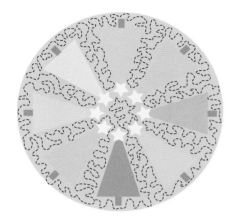

Quilting Diagram

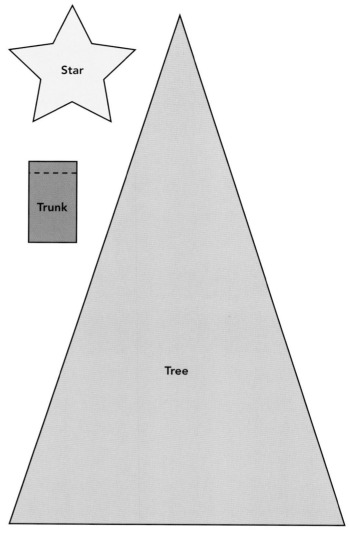

Patterns are shown full size for use with fusible web. Add ³⁄₁₆" seam allowance for hand appliqué.

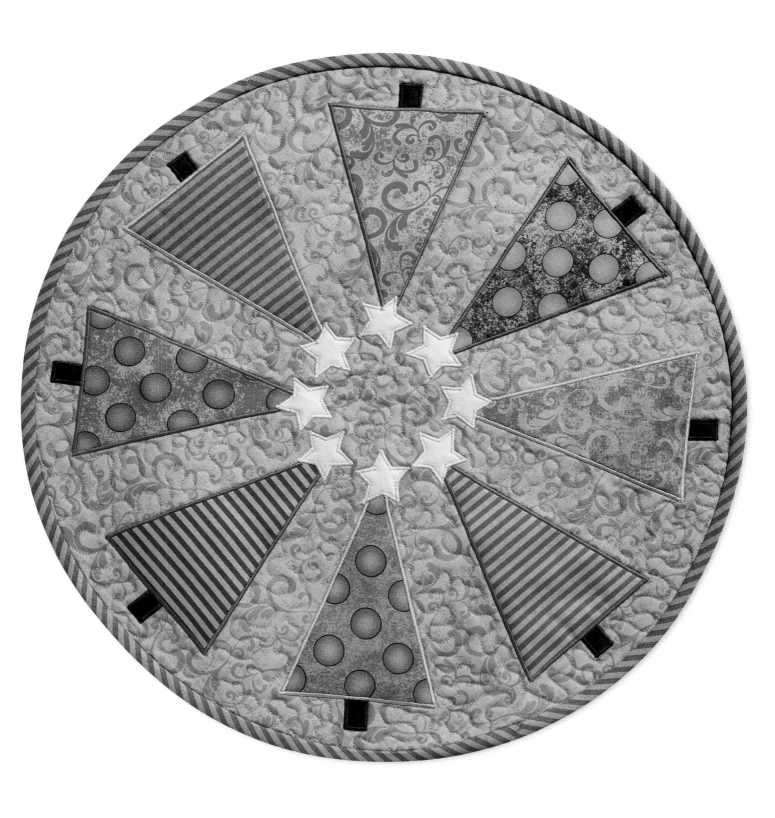

Basic Supplies

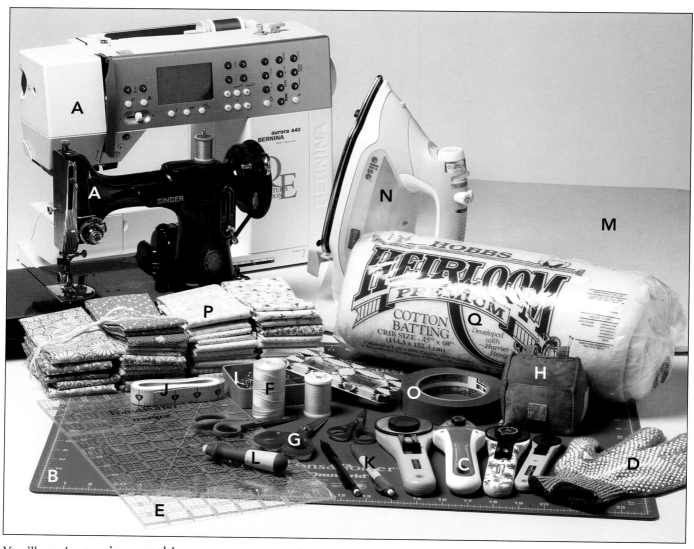

You'll need a **sewing machine (A)** in good working order to construct patchwork blocks, join blocks together, add borders, and machine quilt. We encourage you to purchase a machine from a local dealer, who can help you with service in the future, rather than from a discount store. Another option may be to borrow a machine from a friend or family member. If the machine has not been used in a while, have it serviced by a local dealer to make sure it is in good working order. If you need an extension cord, one with a surge protector is a good idea.

A **rotary cutting mat (B)** is essential for accurate and safe rotary cutting. Purchase one that is no smaller than 18" × 24". Rotary cutting mats are made of "self-healing" material that can be used over and over.

A **rotary cutter (C)** is a cutting tool that looks like a pizza cutter, and has a very sharp blade. We recommend starting with a standard size 45mm rotary cutter. Always lock or close your cutter when it is not in use, and keep it out of the reach of children.

A **safety glove** (also known as a *Klutz Glove)* **(D)** is also recommended. Wear your safety glove on the hand that is holding the ruler in place. Because it is made of cut-resistant material, the safety glove protects your non-cutting hand from accidents that can occur if your cutting hand slips while cutting.

An acrylic **ruler (E)** is used in combination with your cutting mat and rotary cutter. We recommend the Fons & Porter 8" × 14" ruler, but a 6" × 12" ruler is another good option. You'll need a ruler with inch, quarter-inch, and eighth-inch markings that show clearly for ease of measuring. Choose a ruler with 45-degree-angle, 30-degree-angle, and 60-degree-angle lines marked on it as well.

Since you will be using 100% cotton fabric for your quilts, use **cotton or cotton-covered polyester thread (F)** for piecing and quilting. Avoid 100% polyester thread, as it tends to snarl.

Keep a pair of small **scissors (G)** near your sewing machine for cutting threads.

Thin, good-quality **straight pins (H)** are preferred by quilters. The pins included with pincushions are normally too thick to use for piecing, so discard them. Purchase a box of nickel-plated brass **safety pins** size #1 **(I)** to use for pin-basting the layers of your quilt together for machine quilting.

Invest in a 120"-long dressmaker's **measuring tape (J)**. This will come in handy when making borders for your quilt.

A 0.7–0.9mm mechanical **pencil (K)** works well for marking on your fabric.

Invest in a quality, sharp **seam ripper (L)**. Every quilter gets well acquainted with her seam ripper!

Set up an **ironing board (M)** and **iron (N)** in your sewing area. Pressing yardage before cutting, and pressing patchwork seams as you go are both essential for quality quiltmaking. Select an iron that has steam capability.

Masking **tape (O)** or painter's tape works well to mark your sewing machine so you can sew an accurate ¼" seam. You will also use tape to hold your backing fabric taut as you prepare your quilt sandwich for machine quilting.

The most exciting item that you will need for quilting is **fabric (P)**. Quilters generally prefer 100% cotton fabrics for their quilts. This fabric is woven from cotton threads, and has a lengthwise and a crosswise grain. The term "bias" is used to describe the diagonal grain of the fabric. If you make a 45-degree angle cut through a square of cotton fabric, the cut edges will be bias edges, which are quite stretchy. As you learn more quiltmaking techniques, you'll learn how bias can work to your advantage or disadvantage.

Fabric is sold by the yard at quilt shops and fabric stores. Quilting fabric is generally about 40"–44" wide, so a yard is about 40" wide by 36" long. As you collect fabrics to build your own personal stash, you will buy yards, half yards (about 18" × 40"), quarter yards (about 9" × 40"), as well as other lengths.

Many quilt shops sell "fat quarters," a special cut favored by quilters. A fat quarter is created by cutting a half yard down the fold line into two 18" × 20" pieces (fat quarters) that are sold separately. Quilters like the nearly square shape of the fat quarter because it is more useful than the narrow regular quarter yard cut.

Batting (Q) is the filler between quilt top and backing that makes your quilt a quilt. It can be cotton, polyester, cotton-polyester blend, wool, silk, or other natural materials, such as bamboo or corn. Make sure the batting you buy is at least six inches wider and six inches longer than your quilt top.

SEW easy™ Techniques

Quick Triangle-Squares

Use this quick technique to make the triangle-squares for *Fluttering By* on page 14. The Fons & Porter Quarter Inch Seam Marker offers a neat way to mark accurate sewing lines for this method.

1. From each of 2 fabrics, cut 1 square ⅞" larger than the desired finished size of the triangle-square. For example, to make a triangle-square that will finish 1½", as in the *Fluttering By* quilt on page 14, cut 2⅜" squares.

2. On wrong side of lighter square, place the Quarter Inch Seam Marker diagonally across the square, with the yellow center line positioned exactly at opposite corners. Mark stitching lines along both sides of the Quarter Inch Seam Marker *(Photo A)*.

3. Place light square atop darker square, right sides facing; stitch along both marked sewing lines.

4. Cut between rows of stitching to make 2 triangle-squares *(Photo B)*.

SEW easy™

Quick Hourglass Units

Try our quick and easy method to make Hourglass Units without cutting triangles.
The Fons & Porter Quarter Inch Seam Marker helps you draw stitching lines quickly.

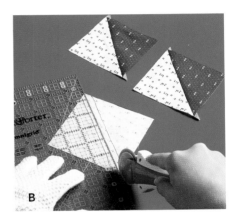

1. From 1 light and 1 dark fabric, cut 1 square 1¼" larger than the desired finished size of the Hourglass Unit. For example, to make an Hourglass Unit that will finish 2" for *Hourglass Runner* on page 34, cut 3¼" squares.

2. Place Quarter Inch Seam Marker diagonally across wrong side of light square, with yellow center line positioned exactly at corners. Mark stitching guidelines along both sides of Quarter Inch Seam Marker *(Photo A)*.

   NOTE: If you are not using the Fons & Porter Quarter Inch Seam Marker, draw a diagonal line from corner to corner across square. Then draw sewing lines on each side of the first line, ¼" away.

3. Place light square atop dark square, right sides facing; stitch along marked sewing lines.

4. Cut between rows of stitching to make two triangle-squares *(Photo B)*. Press seams toward darker fabric.

5. On wrong side of one triangle-square, place Quarter Inch Seam Marker diagonally across square, perpendicular to seam, aligning yellow center line with corners of square. Mark stitching guidelines along both sides of Quarter Inch Seam Marker *(Photo C)*. See note in #2 if you are not using the Fons & Porter Quarter Inch Seam Marker.

6. Place triangle-square with drawn line atop matching triangle-square, right sides and opposite fabrics facing. Stitch along both drawn lines. Cut between rows of stitching to create 2 Hourglass Units *(Photo D)*. Press seam allowances to 1 side.

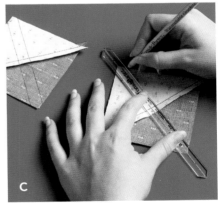

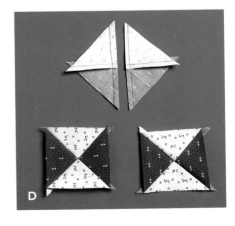

SEW easy™

Paper Foundation Piecing

Paper foundation piecing is ideal for designs with odd angles and sizes of pieces.

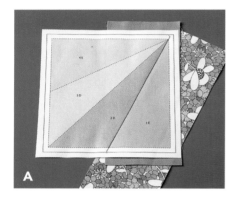

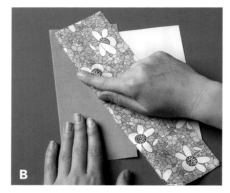

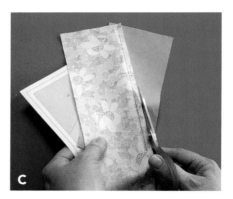

1. Using ruler and pencil, trace all lines and the outer edge of the foundation pattern onto tracing paper. Number the pieces to indicate the stitching order.

Sew Smart™
Save time by making photocopies on special foundation papers. Check photocopied patterns to be sure they are correct size. (Some copiers may distort copy size.) —Liz

2. Using fabric pieces that are larger than the numbered areas, place fabrics for #1 and #2 right sides together. Position paper pattern atop fabrics with printed side of paper facing you. Make sure the fabric for #1 is under that area and that edges of fabrics extend ¼" beyond stitching line between the two sections.

3. Using a short machine stitch so papers will tear off easily later, stitch on line between the two areas, extending stitching into seam allowances at ends of seams *(Photo A)*.

4. Open out pieces and press or finger press the seam *(Photo B)*. The right sides of the fabric pieces will be facing out on the back side of the paper pattern.

5. Flip the work over and fold back paper pattern on stitched line. Trim seam allowance to ¼", being careful not to cut paper pattern *(Photo C)*.

6. Continue to add pieces in numerical order until pattern is covered. Use rotary cutter and ruler to trim excess paper and fabric along outer pattern lines *(Photo D)*.

7. Carefully tear off foundation paper after blocks are joined.

SEW easy™

Windowing Fusible Appliqué

Try our method for utilizing fusible web that
keeps appliqués soft and flexible.

Choose a lightweight "sewable" fusible product. The staff at your favorite quilt shop can recommend brands. Always read and follow manufacturer's instructions for proper fusing time and iron temperature.

Sew Smart™

Fused shapes will be the reverse of the pattern you trace. If it's important for an object to face a certain direction, make a reverse pattern to trace. We do this quickly by tracing the design on tracing paper, then turning the paper over and tracing the design through onto the other side of the paper. —Marianne

1. Trace appliqué motifs onto paper side of fusible web, making a separate tracing for each appliqué needed *(Photo A)*.
2. Roughly cut out drawn appliqué shapes, cutting about ¼" outside drawn lines *(Photo B)*.
3. "Window" the fusible by trimming out the interior of the shape, leaving a scant ¼" inside drawn line *(Photo C)*. Follow manufacturer's instructions

to fuse web side of each shape to wrong side of appliqué fabric.
4. Cut out appliqués, cutting carefully on drawn outline *(Photo D)*. Only a thin band of fusible web frames the shape.
5. Peel off paper backing *(Photo E)*. Position appliqué in place on background fabric, and follow manufacturer's instructions to fuse shapes in place.

Sew Smart™

If you have trouble peeling off the paper backing, try scoring paper with a pin to give you an edge to begin with. —Liz

A

B

C

D

E

Cutting Large Circles

Make perfect circles of any size using these easy-to-follow instructions.

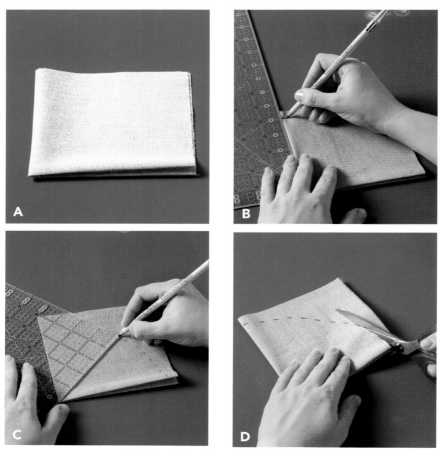

1. Determine diameter of desired circle and cut a square slightly larger than that measurement.
2. Fold square into quarters *(Photo A)*.
3. Divide circle diameter measurement in half to determine radius of circle. Measure that distance from inner point of square and make mark on both edges *(Photo B)*.
4. Rotate ruler and make additional marks *(Photo C)*.
5. Cut folded square along marks *(Photo D)*.